fashion
sourcebooks

The 1970s

John Peacock

Fashion Sourcebooks The 1970s

With 298 illustrations

Thames & Hudson

For Catherine Lamb

First published in the
United Kingdom in 1997 by
Thames & Hudson Ltd,
181A High Holborn,
London WC1V 7QX

www.thamesandhudson.com

Reprinted 2003

British Library Cataloguing-
in-Publication Data
A catalogue record for this book is
available from the British Library.

ISBN 0-500-27972-1

Printed and bound in Slovenia by
Mladinska Knjiga

Contents

In the 1970s, advances in production technology enabled clothing manufacturers to plan ahead, ensuring a uniformity of style, finish and cost, and making standard off-the-peg garments available everywhere, in all colours and sizes.

Ready-to-wear clothing at the beginning of the 1970s was classic. The look for women was streamlined, well cut, clean and unfussy; the look for men was similar: sleek, long-line jackets with wide lapels, teamed with flared trousers. As the decade progressed, women's clothes retained their classic, well-tailored appearance, though they became more closely fitted to the body, and skirts lengthened. Fashion details included buttoned-down flap pockets, long collars, tight sleeves with deep cuffs and wide, hip-level belts. Women began to wear trousers more often and for more varied occasions. Trouser suits, in a wide variety of fabrics from crushed velvet to linen tweed, became popular. Fabrics with a matt surface were most in vogue: brushed cottons, cotton velvets, wool jersey, and real and imitation suede.

Both bright colours and more subtle and subdued shades were fashionable. Bright colours were worn alone or combined with others; for example, canary yellow was teamed with dark brown and grey; lilac with purple and pink; slate grey, dull turquoise and terracotta were worn with black.

Many of the decade's younger and more unconventional women and men wanted to break away from what was on offer in the high street from well-known manufacturers and designers, and as the 1970s progressed their dress became increasingly individualistic. Though they still wore mass-produced clothing, it was often mixed with clothes from past decades and other cultures. National costumes, slinky day and evening wear from the 1930s (the Biba look), and Carmen Miranda 1940s platform shoes were worn by women alongside ethnic shawls and embroidered shirts from Greece and Turkey, and sequined silks and gold jewelry from India. Nor were men immune to these trends: a not untypical seventies look comprised an eighteenth-century-style frilled shirt, a multicoloured embroidered ethnic waistcoat and velvet trousers tucked into knee-high riding boots. Any one of these elements could also be teamed with off-the-peg garments.

In the main, the fashions I have illustrated here are such as would be worn by the middle or upper-middle classes and by people who would have had a keen interest in the latest styles, while not being 'dedicated followers of fashion'. It therefore follows that I have not included many of the more idiosyncratic outfits described above.

Men's fashions, as always, moved more slowly than women's, though the 1970s witnessed a more obvious change in design detail than previous decades. The suit still dominated, but with subtle changes to jacket fit and shape, length, button fastening and the width of lapels, which grew almost to cover the chest towards the close of the decade. Trousers also changed shape, often made without pockets to obtain the much-desired smooth hipline and with hems flaring to cover platform-soled shoes. Hand-knitted jackets and cardigans in bright colours and bold patterns, with shawl collars and tie belts, were much worn for leisure activities. The ideal shirt at the beginning of the seventies was fitted, pastel coloured and had a long pointed collar, and was teamed with a wide, boldly patterned, brightly coloured 'kipper' tie. By the decade's end it had changed to a baggy, subtly coloured, linen-tweed garment with a tiny collar, worn with a narrow leather tie. These

differences and the basic trends in men's fashion have been shown, on average, with one example on each page.

The sources from which I have drawn – chiefly from Great Britain, North America, France, Italy and Germany – include contemporary magazines, catalogues and journals, original dated photographs, museum collections, and my own costume collection.

This Sourcebook is divided into ten sections, each of which includes four subdivisions covering Day Wear, Evening Wear (alternately, on two occasions, Wedding Wear), Sports and Leisure Wear, and a section on either Underwear and Negligee or Accessories. Following the main illustrations are ten pages of schematic drawings accompanied by detailed notes about each example, giving particulars of colour, cut and trimming as well as other useful information. Then follow two pages of drawings which illustrate the decade 'at a glance' and which demonstrate the evolution of the period and its main development trends.

Biographies of the most important international fashion designers of the decade are also included as well as a list of further reading suggestions into the styles of this period.

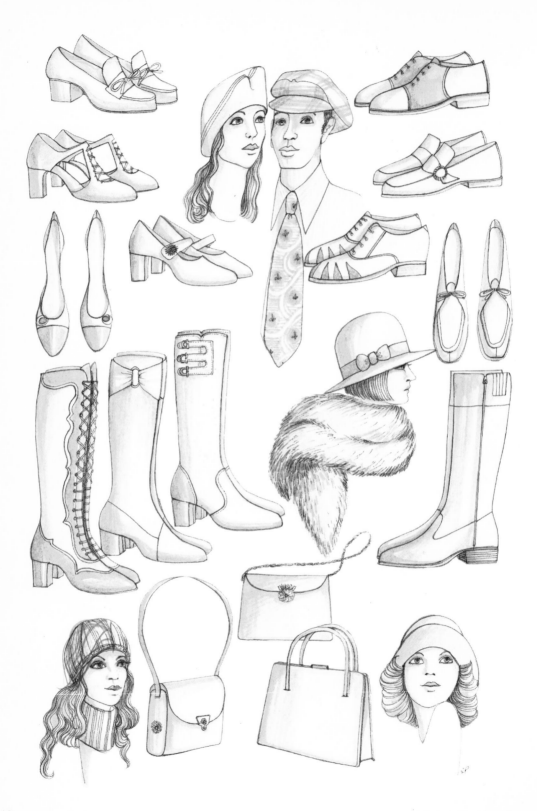

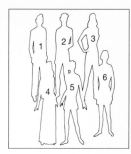

1970 Day Wear

1 Two-piece grey and maroon checked wool suit: hip-length single-breasted jacket, fastening from above hemline to under shirt collar, large black silk bow trim, long inset sleeves, split at wrist-level, button trim, wide black patent-leather belt, large buckle, hip-level flap pockets, button trim; flared mini skirt, wide box-pleats. Black leather gloves. Black patent-leather bar-strap shoes, low thick heels. 2 Two-piece dark-grey and navy-blue flecked wool-tweed suit: single-breasted jacket, high three-button fastening, narrow lapels, shaped flap pockets, top-stitched edges and detail; straight-cut trousers, no turn-ups. Blue cotton collar-attached shirt. Blue and grey striped silk tie. Black leather step-in shoes. 3 Double-breasted cream wool-gabardine midi-length coat, outsized lapels, large collar, bolero cut in one with bodice, long inset sleeves, buttoned strap above wrist, self-fabric belt, round brown plastic buckle, matching buttons, hip-level patch pockets, flared skirts. Cream wool polo-neck sweater. Brown felt fedora, high crown, brown band, wide brim. Brown plastic knee-high boots, fitted legs, thick heels. 4 Unfitted grey flannel dress, buttoned-strap fastening from hip-level to under shirt collar, long inset sleeves gathered into deep cuffs in navy-blue flannel, matching shoulder yoke and small plastic buttons, mini skirt. Knee-length navy-blue leather boots, fitted legs, thick heels. 5 Brown velvet jumpsuit, semi-fitted bodice, buttoned-strap fastening from bust-level to under high round neckline, zip fastening under strap to crotch, long inset sleeves, deep cuffs, trousers fitted over hips, hip-level vertical welt pockets set into central seam on front, flared legs from low hip-level to hem, top-stitched edges and detail. Yellow velvet cap, gathered crown, large peak. Yellow plastic clogs, blunt toes, wooden soles.

Evening Wear

1 Two-piece black mohair and silk evening suit: single-breasted fitted jacket, high two-button fastening, narrow silk-faced lapels, matching covered buttons, fine bound pockets; narrow trousers, no turn-ups. White silk shirt worn with wing collar. Narrow black silk bow-tie. Black patent-leather step-in shoes, blunt toes. 2 Ankle-length semi-fitted black silk-chiffon evening dress, high polo-neck, long inset sleeves, right sleeve and right side front and back of dress beaded and embroidered in yellow, gold and green from shoulder to hem of straight skirt, dress worn over black silk slip. Black satin boots, blunt toes, high heels. 3 Multicoloured paisley-patterned evening pyjamas: strapless hip-length smocked bodice; wide flared trousers gathered from hip-level. Black and yellow glass bead necklace: jabot of glass flowers hanging from fine gold chains. Black satin shoes, large square jeweled buckles, blunt toes. 4 Cocktail ensemble: silver ribbon-embroidered lace hip-length top, low V-shaped neckline, scalloped edges matching hemline and edges of long inset sleeves; multilayered pink and grey silk-chiffon mini-length skirt gathered from hip-level. Silver stretch-Lurex tights. Silver kid sling-back shoes, blunt toes decorated with self-kid flower, low square heels. 5 Purple crushed-velvet cocktail dress, fitted bodice worn open at front and laced from high round neckline to waist-level with black satin laces, cut-away armholes, mini-length skirt gathered from waist. Black stretch-lace tights. Black satin bar-strap shoes, blunt toes, high thick heels.

Sports and Leisure Wear

1 Holiday wear. All-in-one crocheted pink cotton jumpsuit, semi-fitted hip-length bodice, front zip fastening from hip-level to under high round neckline, cut-away armholes, trousers flared from knee-level. Pink leather shoes, top-stitched detail, blunt toes, low thick heels. 2 Beach wear. White knitted-cotton T-shirt, high round neckline trimmed with bands of red and navy-blue to match cuffs of long inset sleeves and hip-level band, manufacturer's logo on side chest. Fitted dark-blue cotton shorts, fly fastening, logo matching one on shirt on side front hem. 3 Swim wear. Swim trunks in multicoloured patterned stretch-nylon, red elasticated-nylon belt threaded through self-fabric loops on hipline, large round clasp fastening. 4 Cycling. Turquoise knitted-wool hip-length sweater, ribbed edge of low round neckline knitted in pale-coffee, matching cut-away armholes, inset band under bust also edged with brown, repeated over ribbed hem, appliqué gold star over left breast. Pale-turquoise synthetic-crepe blouse, long pointed collar, button fastening, long inset sleeves gathered into buttoned cuffs. Dark-turquoise cotton fitted shorts. Flesh-coloured nylon tights. Turquoise, beige and brown knitted-wool beret. Knee-high brown leather fitted boots, blunt toes, flat heels. 5 Beach wear. Fine yellow cotton crocheted bikini: small bra top, cups linked at front by wooden ring covered in matching cotton, back fastening, fine halter-straps fastening at back of neck; tiny briefs in matching fabric. Large yellow and white canvas bag, top-stitched detail. Yellow canvas pumps, round toes, bow trim, flat heels.

Underwear and Negligee

1 Red cotton pyjamas: hip-length single-breasted jacket, four-pearl-button fastening from waist to under shirt collar, long inset sleeves, stitched cuffs piped in white to match edge of front opening, collar and hip-level welt pockets; trousers with elasticated waist, legs slightly flared, no turn-ups. Red leather slippers, flat heels. 2 White knitted-cotton T-shirt, high round neckline with stitched edge matching hems of short inset sleeves. White knitted-cotton underpants, Y-front opening, elasticated waistband. 3 Beige nylon and Lycra bodysuit, moulded and seamed bra top, elasticated and adjustable shoulder straps, panelled body, high-cut legs. 4 Lime-green nylon nightdress, low V-shaped neckline and cut-away armholes edged with fine pale-coffee nylon lace, neckline trimmed above point with tiny self-fabric rouleau bow, ground-length gathered skirt falls from deep inset band of smocking under bust which also provides shaping under bust. Lime-green satin pumps. 5 Combination bodysuit and slip, pale-pink and black stretch-nylon lace bodice, unstructured bra top, elasticated and adjustable shoulder straps, pink nylon mini-length skirt falls from hip seam curved front and back. 6 Pink nylon and Lycra bra, moulded, seamed and darted cups, removable wire supports, pale-coffee nylon lace trim, elasticated and adjustable shoulder straps, back fastening. Pink nylon flared mini-length slip, elasticated waist, scalloped hemline trimmed with wide pale-coffee nylon lace.

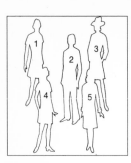

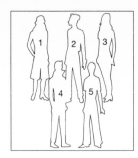

1971 Day Wear

1 Semi-fitted blue-grey wool dress, high round neckline bound in tan to match shaped bindings on short inset sleeves, shaped inset bands of tan and cream above waistline and on shoulders, knee-length flared skirt. Black plastic knee-high fitted boots, round toes. **2** Pale-blue denim single-breasted jacket, two-button fastening, wide lapels, large patch pockets, shaped flaps, top-stitched edges and seams. Dark-pink cotton trousers, flared from above knee-level, no turn-ups. Deep-pink knitted-wool polo-neck sweater. Brown shiny plastic ankle-boots, blunt toes, stacked heels. **3** Dark-grey wool coat, single-breasted buttoned-strap fastening from low hip-level to under large collar and lapels, buttoned shoulder yoke, long cuffed sleeves, self-fabric tie-belt, vertical welt pockets in knee-length flared skirts, top-stitched edges and seams. Blue and brown striped silk scarf. Grey felt hat, tall crown, dark ribbon band, wide brim. Knee-high black leather boots, strap-and-buckle trim, blunt toes. **4** Cream wool dress, semi-fitted black and cream patchwork bodice trimmed with silver studs, high round neckline, short inset sleeves, mini-length flared skirt, centre-front seam split six inches above hemline, black leather belt, silver clasp fastening set with black stone. Black leather shoes, high vamp, round toes, stacked heels. **5** Pale-blue wool coat, semi-fitted bodice, asymmetric fastening, three large horn buttons from waist to under collar of looped wool which matches cuffs of long inset sleeves, vertical welt pockets in knee-length flared skirts, top-stitched edges. Cloche hat in matching fabric. Pale-blue gloves. Dark-blue leather T-strap shoes, round toes.

Evening Wear

1 Black silk-taffeta evening dress, fitted pintucked bodice, black lace yoke and stand collar with matching scalloped edges, elbow-length inset puffed sleeves, frilled cuffs trimmed with ribbon and lace to match hems of two-tier skirt, embroidered and beaded shaped black velvet belt. Black satin shoes, round toes, low thick heels. **2** Tangerine rayon-crepe evening dress, unfitted bodice and ground-length skirt cut in one piece, high waist position marked with gold lamé belt beaded and embroidered in black, full raglan sleeves gathered into edge of low round neckline and into narrow rouleau cuffs. Black satin shoes, round toes, crossed straps. **3** Pale-gold-yellow evening dress, spotted in orange and gold Lurex, high-waisted fitted bodice, fine gold Lurex piping either side of mock-button fastening of self-fabric-covered buttons on centre front, on high waist seam and seam between tight inset upper sleeves and gathered lower sleeves, matching narrow rouleau cuffs, ankle-length flared skirt. Gold kid shoes, round toes, bow trim, low thick heels. **4** Two-piece dark-green silk and mohair evening suit: fitted single-breasted jacket, two-button fastening under low-cut wide satin-covered lapels, deep flap pockets, inset sleeves, single-button trim; flared trousers, braided outer seams, no turn-ups. White silk collar-attached shirt, pintucked either side of fly fastening. Dark-green velvet bow-tie. Black patent-leather elastic-sided boots. **5** Two-piece black wool and silk suit: hip-length fitted single-breasted jacket, single-button fastening under wide satin-faced shawl collar, panel seams from shoulder to hem; wide-flared trousers, no creases or turn-ups. White silk scarf tied in neck of jacket. Black velvet shoes, round toes, high thick heels.

Sports and Leisure Wear

1 Country wear. Short green suede jacket, single-breasted buttoned-strap fastening from above waistband to under pointed shirt collar, side panel seams, patch pockets, inset sleeves, buttoned cuffs, top-stitched edges and seams. Beige, green and white herringbone wool-tweed culottes, flared from hip to knee, pockets set into side seams. Beige wool polo-neck sweater. Brown, green, beige and white knitted-wool hat, padded brim. Knee-high brown leather boots, side zip fastening, thick heels. **2** Ski wear. Yellow nylon suit: waist-length jacket, front zip fastening from above buttoned waistband to under quilted shirt collar, buttoned-down points, quilted side panels with zipped pockets, long inset sleeves, buttoned strap above hem; fitted trousers, front zip opening, matching vertical pockets and side opening, quilted front panels. Knitted red and yellow striped hood. Red and yellow leather gloves. Red leather ski boots. **3** Holiday wear. Blue brushed-cotton fitted hip-length T-shirt, wide round neckline, short inset sleeves, wide leather belt, metal buckle, decorative studs. Fitted shorts to match T-shirt. Beige leather lace-up shoes, thick heels. **4** Ski wear. Red nylon suit: short jacket, fake fur front and back, matching collar, front zip fastening, inset sleeves; quilted trousers, zipped vertical pockets and side openings. Black wool polo-neck sweater. Red nylon hood. Red and black padded leather gloves. Black leather ski boots. **5** Holiday wear. Blue and white broken striped knitted-cotton shirt, zip fastening, pointed collar, flap pockets, short inset sleeves, edges and detail outlined in yellow. White synthetic linen-look trousers, waistband with buckle fastening, fitted over hips, piped pockets, flared from knee, no turn-ups. White leather step-in shoes, top-stitched detail.

Accessories

1 Dark-green leather shoes, high vamp, bow trim, low thick heels. **2** Pink wool beret, top-stitched detail. **3** Large checked wool cap. Striped shirt, long pointed collar. Wide 'kipper' tie, bold pattern. **4** Green and cream lace-up leather shoes, man-made soles and heels. **5** Black leather shoes, cut-away sides, open fronts with decorative lacing, round toes, high thick heels. **6** Pink grosgrain evening shoes, bar-strap, decorative clasp fastening, medium-high thick heels. **7** White leather shoes, red trim and laces, thick man-made soles and stacked heels. **8** White leather step-in shoes, high tongues, buckle trim, man-made soles and heels. **9** Grey leather shoes, black patent-leather toecaps and asymmetric buckle trim, round toes. **10** Beige suede shoes, leather laces, top-stitched seams. **11** Knee-high maroon leather lace-up boots, round toes, thick high heels, cream suede uppers, scalloped seams piped in white. **12** Powder-blue suede knee-high boots, self-suede draped band threaded through silver ring below knee-level, round toes, high thick heels. **13** Long tan leather boots, mock strap-and-buckle fastening at knee-level, high thick heels. **14** Mole-grey felt hat, large crown, black ribbon trim, wide brim. Silver fox-fur scarf. **15** Long brown leather boots, side zip fastening, elasticated inserts at knee-level, thick soles, stacked heels. **16** Stone knitted-wool beret. Matching polo-neck sweater. **17** Dark-red leather shoulder bag, flap with gilt-clasp fastening, matching trim on side panel, long handle. **18** Black silk evening bag, flap with jeweled gilt clasp, long gilt-chain handle. **19** Large black patent-leather handbag, metal frame, clasp fastening, double self-leather rouleau handles. **20** Blue felt hat, large crown, turned-back brim.

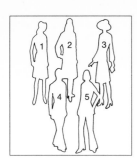
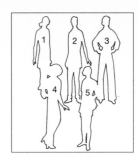
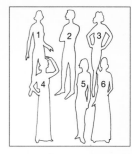

1972 Day Wear

1 Grey and white flecked wool two-piece suit: hip-length single-breasted jacket, small revers, pointed collar, narrow inset sleeves, bust-level mock-flap pockets, hip-level patch pockets with flaps, self-fabric tie-belt, top-stitched edges and detail; knee-length flared skirt. Pale-grey polo-neck sweater. Grey felt hat, twisted black ribbon band. Black leather gloves, matching T-strap shoes, peep toes. **2** Fawn wool coat, buttoned-strap fastening from hem to under large collar, wide batwing sleeves, buttoned cuffs, self-fabric buckled belt, hip-level patch pockets, side opening, mock-flap pockets, button trim, knee-length flared skirts, top-stitched edges and detail. Green and red patterned white silk scarf. White jersey-wool pull-on hat. Knee-high brown suede boots, leather platform soles and thick heels. **3** White cotton dress spotted in black, pointed collar, long sleeves, buttoned cuffs, knee-length box-pleated skirt. Fitted black wool-jersey sweater, scooped neckline, short inset sleeves, gilt-chain belt. Large white straw hat, black ribbon band. White handbag. Black leather sling-back sandals, strap-and-buckle fastening, peep toes, platform soles, thick high heels. **4** Grey and blue checked wool two-piece suit: single-breasted jacket, four-button fastening, narrow lapels, pointed collar, box-pleated patch pockets, buttoned flaps, self-fabric buckled belt; trousers flared from knee, no turn-ups. Pale-grey collar-attached shirt. Blue striped tie. Black leather step-in shoes. **5** Brown and beige checked wool two-piece suit: single-breasted fitted jacket, three-button fastening to under wide lapels, brown velvet collar, matching covered buttons, narrow inset sleeves, four flap pockets; trousers flare from knee-level. Beige wool sweater. Brown leather ankle-boots, round toes, high stacked heels.

Evening Wear

1 Two-piece dinner ensemble: hip-length black sequined top, semi-fitted bodice, inset sleeves gathered into cuffs, deep V-shaped neckline, long silver satin collar, matching cummerbund with large bow trim, vest inset and ankle-length flared skirt. Black satin shoes, square toes. **2** Dusty-pink silk-jersey evening dress, straight-cut bodice and ground-length skirt cut in one piece, gathered into high round neckline and on waist with wide self-fabric sash, long narrow inset sleeves. Matching ground-length scarf. Close-fitting brimless cap, covering hair, embroidered and beaded in pink and silver. Silver kid shoes. **3** Pale-sage-green silk-satin two-piece evening pyjama suit: hip-length shirt-style jacket, single-breasted buttoned-strap fastening from hemline to under long pointed collar, narrow inset sleeves gathered into buttoned cuffs, self-fabric tie-belt, large hip-level patch pockets, top-stitched edges and detail; wide ground-length trousers, gathered from waist. Silver kid shoes. **4** Cream wool dinner dress, fitted bodice, slashed neckline, inset sleeves, flared hems decorated with inset bands of black wool to match hemline of ankle-length flared skirt and single band above waist seam. Black satin sling-back shoes, square toes, high thick heels. **5** Two-piece hostess ensemble: hip-length lilac wool-jersey top, high round neckline, deep armholes and hemline edged in purple, matching narrow suede belt; ankle-length black wool-jersey dress patterned with blue, lilac, purple and pink butterflies in various sizes, high polo-neck collar, inset sleeves gathered into buttoned cuffs, ankle-length flared skirt. Purple satin mules, peep toes, high platform soles and wedge heels.

Sports and Leisure Wear

1 Golf. Sage-green knitted-cotton shirt, front zip fastening to under long pointed collar, matching diagonal piped pockets above waist, short inset sleeves. Pink and green checked polyester mini-length flared skirt, no waistband, centre-front inverted box-pleat, two large hip-level patch pockets cut on bias. White leather step-in shoes, fringed tongues, blunt toes, flat heels. **2** Tennis. White rayon semi-fitted sleeveless dress, pintucked bib front, mock-strap opening to under wide round neckline, mini-length flared skirt. White cotton-towelling sweatband, matching wristband. White cotton ankle-socks. White canvas training shoes. **3** Country wear. Beige bouclé knitted-polyester jacket, front zip fastening from hem of deep ribbed waistband to ends of matching ribbed turned-down collar, wide batwing sleeves gathered into ribbed cuffs. Fitted grey flannel trousers, flared knee-level to hem, no turn-ups, central creases. Beige and grey knitted-polyester ribbed pull-on hat. Leather ankle-boots, square toes, top-stitched detail. **4** Holiday wear. White knitted-cotton two-piece patterned with uneven stripes of pink, turquoise, green and pale-blue: cropped top, low round neckline, short inset sleeves, top-stitched edges; hipster trousers, no hipband, wide legs, no turn-ups or creases. Large white straw hat. White leather sling-back sandals, strap fronts, blunt toes. **5** Holiday wear. Two-piece cotton-polyester beach suit: long bright-turquoise shirt, short inset sleeves, dark-blue buttoned-strap fastening from hem to under long pointed collar, worn open, matching shoulder yoke buttoned onto shaped patch pockets, patch pockets with mock-buttoned flaps and buttoned waistband of shorts.

Underwear and Negligee

1 White crochet-look nylon-doubleknit bra, moulded underwired cups, elasticated adjustable shoulder straps, back fastening. White nylon-doubleknit panty-girdle, shaped waist, top-stitched tummy control panel, long legs, elasticated nylon lace trim. **2** One-piece waist-to-toe grey wool undergarment, elasticated waistband, white cotton crotch panel, side opening, fitted legs incorporating knee-high ribbed dress socks. **3** Cream stretch-nylon body-shirt incorporating short panties, button opening from bust-level to under high round neckline, short inset sleeves, high-cut legs, fastening under crotch. **4** Pale-blue nylon sleeveless nightdress, low V-shaped neckline to high waistline marked by nylon-cord double-belt, large bow tied at front, bodice and ground-length skirt cut in one piece. **5** Black machine-embroidered cotton two-piece underwear set: unstructured bra, low V-shaped neckline, bow trim, adjustable satin-ribbon shoulder straps, back fastening; hipster briefs, elasticated waist and high-cut legs. **6** Ground-length nightdress, sleeveless high-waisted peach silk bodice, self-fabric-covered button trim under low V-shaped neckline, deep armholes, narrow cut-away shoulders, flared yellow silk skirt, centre-front inverted box-pleat, edges bound in silk to match bodice.

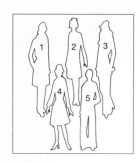
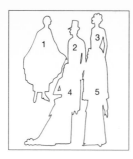
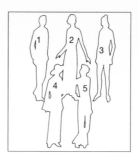

1973 Day Wear

1 White wool two-piece suit: knee-length wrapover coat, large white fur shawl collar, long inset sleeves, self-fabric tie-belt, hip-level pockets; straight-cut trousers, creases, no turn-ups. White felt hat, high crown, wide brim. White leather ankle-boots, platform soles, high thick heels.
2 Cream wool-crepe dress, brown cord-velvet shaped yoke, two self-fabric-covered buttons, wide-set collar, short inset sleeves, shaped cuffs, matching trim on hip-level offset patch pockets, semi-fitted bodice and flared skirt cut in one piece, top-stitched edges and detail. Brown velvet hairband, bow trim. Brown leather shoes, platform soles.
3 Grey and red flecked wool-tweed two-piece suit: long double-breasted jacket, wide lapels, large collar worn turned up, long inset sleeves, stitched cuffs, self-fabric buckled belt, welt pockets; wide flared trousers, top-stitched edges and detail. Red polyester blouse, long pointed collar. Hat in tweed to match suit, sectioned crown, narrow brim. Grey leather gloves; matching ankle-boots, blunt toes, platform soles, high thick heels.
4 White polyester dress spotted in red, semi-fitted bodice, high round neckline, self-fabric scarf tied on one side, flower trim, long inset sleeves, buttoned cuffs, self-fabric buckled belt, skirt fitted over hips, flared from hip to knee-level. Outsized bowler-style hat in fabric matching dress, high crown, wide band, narrow curled brim. Red leather bar-strap shoes, high thick heels.
5 Dark-brown leather jacket, front zip fastening, pointed collar, high yoke seam, mock-flap pockets, patch pockets with mock flaps and side opening, inset sleeves, ribbed-wool cuffs, matching waistband. Brown wool polo-neck sweater. Light-brown wool-flannel fitted trousers, wide flares from above knee, no turn-ups. Brown leather ankle-boots, platform soles.

Wedding Wear

1 Cream cotton-lawn wedding dress, large oval cape, mock bodice with boat-shaped neckline, pintucks and lace trim, sham-strap opening, self-fabric-covered buttons, bodice held by threaded lace-covered self-fabric belt at high-waist position, outside and inside edges of cape trimmed with bias-cut cream satin ribbon and lace, matching trim on ankle-length skirt. Close-fitting cream cotton-lawn bonnet, trimmed lace, fastening under chin. Cream leather ankle-strap shoes, cut-away detail above high thick heels and platform soles.
2 Formal wedding attire: fitted single-breasted grey wool tailcoat, single-button fastening, wide lapels, breast pocket, silk handkerchief. Single-breasted collarless pale-grey wool waistcoat. Black and grey striped wool trousers, straight-cut, no turn-ups. White shirt, imperial collar; black, grey and white striped silk cravat; pin. Grey top hat. Black shoes.
3 White nylon wedding dress, random white nylon-lace appliqué flower decoration on fitted bodice, tight sleeves and full gathered skirt, frilled hem, scalloped neckline and sleeve hems; strapless white nylon-taffeta under-dress. Wreath of fresh flowers worn as headdress. Matching bouquet.
4 Matt-ivory silk-satin pinafore-style wedding dress, low scooped neckline, fitted bodice and ground-length skirt cut in one piece, bias-cut waterfall frill set into side seams, continues around long train, large bow trim at back, pearl- and crystal-embroidered blouse, long tight sleeves, high round neckline. Long tulle veil attached to hair ornament. 5 Cream wool-crepe wedding dress, semi-fitted, flared from under bust to ground-length hem, no waist seam, low scooped neckline under bust, infilled to high round neckline, infill matching cuffs of sleeves and close-fitting brimless cap. Cream leather shoes.

Sports and Leisure Wear

1 Casual wear. Green collarless machine-knitted cardigan-jacket, single-breasted button fastening, ribbed edges in brown and cream matching cuffs of long inset sleeves and tops of patch pockets, wide self-colour rib inset on waistline. Green machine-knitted sleeveless sweater, V-shaped neckline. Green-grey flannel trousers, flared hems, no turn-ups. Brown brushed-cotton collar-attached shirt. Brown, green and cream checked cravat. Brown leather ankle-boots.
2 Holiday wear. Two-piece multicoloured spotted cotton beach suit: semi-fitted cropped top, cut-away armholes, high roll collar, long V-shaped slash from neckline to under bust; trousers cut without waistband, fitted over hips, wide flared legs; turban in matching fabric. Leather sandals, low wedge heels, peep toes.
3 Yoga. Grey knitted mini dress with built-in briefs, wide shoulder straps, fitted bodice, tiny flared skirt, white leather hip-belt, stud fastening, detachable purse.
4 Casual/Country wear. Two-piece green wool-flannel suit: short single-breasted jacket, button fastening, small revers, large collar, long inset sleeves, buttoned strap above wrist, patch pockets, buttoned flaps, self-fabric belt, round buckle, top-stitched edges and detail; trousers fitted over hips, flared from knee-level to hem, central creases. Dark-green wool polo-neck sweater. Rust-brown suede hat, sectioned crown. Brown leather shoulder bag; matching ankle-boots. 5 Casual wear. Blue denim dungarees, bib front, central patch pocket, adjustable shoulder straps, inset waistband, patch pockets either side fly-front fastening, fitted over hips, wide flares, multicoloured machine-embroidery. Gold panne-velvet top, high round neckline, long inset sleeves gathered into bow-tied rouleau bands. Gold kid boots, peep toes, high thick heels.

Accessories

1 Red and black crocheted-wool pull-on hat. Red, black, green and cream patterned crocheted-wool scarf, tasselled hem.
2 Burgundy leather bag, flap, clasp fastening, long handle.
3 Brown mock-patent-leather bag, flap, clasp fastening, small handle, long detachable rouleau handle. 4 Outsized pink suede peaked cap. 5 Small beige leather clutch bag, black patent panel in flap, zipped pockets, wrist handle. 6 Blue and red canvas lace-up shoes, platform soles, thick heels. 7 Shiny green leather shoulder bag, long handle, flap with applied matt-leather trim, clasp fastening.
8 Red silk-jersey turban. Plastic amber necklace and clip-on earrings. 9 Cream canvas shoes, green leather platform soles, low thick heels and strap trim.
10 Green patent-leather shoes, high tongues, strap-and-buckle trim, blunt toes, low thick heels.
11 Black patent-leather shoes, low-cut front and sides, metal trim on blunt toes and above low thick heels. 12 Shiny red leather shoes, ankle straps, buckle fastening, open sides, high straight heels. 13 Red waterproofed-cotton hat, top-stitched sectioned crown, matching wide brim. 14 Green snakeskin shoes, platform soles, high shaped heels, inset black suede trim on uppers. 15 Black and white patent-leather shoes, perforated detail, high thick heels.
16 Blue mock-suede sports visor, wide band edged in cream, matching outsized visor.
17 Yellow plastic mules, high pointed vamp, flared heels.
18 Cream leather sling-back shoes, peep toes, powder-blue platform soles and flared heels.
19 Knee-high brown suede boots, platform soles, high straight heels, side zip fastening.
20 Above-knee-high blue leather boots, platform soles, flared heels. 21 Tan leather beret.
22 Silver Lurex pull-on hat. Fox fur. 23 Blue felt hat, self-felt trim.

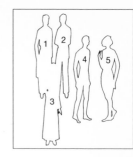

1974 Day Wear

1 Green wool two-piece suit: long single-breasted jacket, wide lapels, long inset sleeves, welt pockets, edges and detail finished with rows of machine top-stitching, green leather belt, matching covered buttons; knee-length flared skirt. Green satin blouse, tie at neck with rows of machine top-stitching. White and green wool-jersey turban-style hat. Green leather bag; matching shoes, ankle straps, cut-away sides, high heels. 2 Coffee rayon thirties-style dress patterned with multicoloured flowers, semi-fitted bodice, buttoned-strap opening, self-fabric belt, low sweetheart neckline, gathers from centre-front bust, short puffed sleeves, narrow skirt to below knee-level. Yellow lacquered-straw hat, white daisy trim. White gloves. Coffee leather shoes, double ankle straps, high thick heels. 3 Light-tan wool-flannel suit: single-breasted fitted jacket, three-button fastening, wide lapels, patch pockets, top-stitched mock flaps, matching edges and detail; flared trousers, deep turn-ups. Dark-tan cotton shirt, attached collar with long points. Cream, brown and tan patterned silk tie; matching breast pocket handkerchief. Leather ankle-boots. 4 Blue wool four-piece suit: long unfitted single-breasted collarless jacket, buttons in sets of three, edges bound with coffee, brown and cream zigzag-patterned wool to match welt pockets, hems of long inset sleeves, flared and pleated skirt and long scarf; collarless single-breasted waistcoat, self-fabric binding. Coffee lacquered-straw hat. Coffee leather bag and shoes. 5 Single-breasted mid-calf-length grey and yellow flecked showerproof wool-tweed coat, flared from shoulders, horn buttons, large shirt collar, long inset cuffed sleeves, diagonal welt pockets. Wide grey flannel trousers, no creases or turn-ups. Grey wool beret. Grey leather shoes, stacked heels.

Evening Wear

1 Midnight-blue silk-jersey evening dress, wide halter-straps form cross-over backless bodice, open V-shape on centre-front above wide draped cummerbund, floor-length gathered skirt, centre-front wide-spaced unpressed inverted box-pleat. Midnight-blue satin strap sandals. 2 Single-breasted fitted red velvet jacket, single-button fastening under wide lapels, fitted sleeves, large patch pockets. Collarless single-breasted black silk waistcoat, low V-shaped neckline, pointed hem. Flared black wool trousers, no turn-ups. White silk collar-attached shirt, buttoned-strap fastening. Large black silk bow-tie. Black suede ankle-boots. 3 White silk-crepe thirties-style evening dress, bias-cut bodice and floor-length flared skirt cut in one piece without waist seam, wide godets set into hem of side seams, upper bodice draped over bust on either side centre-front seam, fine self-fabric rouleau halter straps from centre of shaped neckline. Draped turban in matching fabric, bead brooch trim. White shoes. 4 Floor-length navy-blue and silver synthetic-chiffon evening dress overprinted in pink and white, full-length cape sleeves cut in one piece with bodice from high round neckline, narrow belt, bow trim, gathered skirt, navy-blue synthetic-silk underdress, fitted bodice, high round neckline, cut-away armholes, gathered skirt. Navy-blue silk shoes, peep toes, low platform soles. 5 White silk-chiffon evening dress printed with outsized red and pink poppies and golden corn, fitted bodice mounted over white silk, low scooped neckline, full-length unlined inset sleeves gathered into rouleau bands, wide waist sash, large black silk poppy trim on side waist above trailing ends, ground-length gathered skirt, underskirt of same shape. Red silk shoes.

Leisure Wear

1 Holiday wear. Two-piece white cotton beach suit patterned with red, yellow and orange berries and outsized green leaves: cropped top, cut-away armholes gathered into plain orange cotton binding around high round neckline; mid-calf-length flared skirt, plain orange cotton tie-belt. Lime-green headscarf tied into large bow on one side. Plastic jewelry in bright colours. Multicoloured plastic strap sandals, thick cork platform soles. 2 Holiday wear. Pale-green cotton-poplin beach dress patterned with bands of multicoloured flowers, four-tier mid-calf-length skirt gathered from high yoke, wide shoulder straps. Dark-green canvas beach shoes, low wedge heels, thin platform soles. 3 Holiday wear. Waist-length yellow knitted-wool single-breasted waistcoat, three-button fastening, front edges finished with dark-yellow rib to match armholes, tops of patch pockets and hem. Cream cotton flared trousers, side hip pockets, no turn-ups. Orange cotton shirt, pointed collar worn open, short inset cuffed sleeves. Tan and white leather step-in shoes. 4 Holiday wear. Red, white and black striped cotton shirt, pointed collar worn open, long fitted cuffed inset sleeves. White knitted-cotton sleeveless sweater, red and black stripes from above waist-level rib to under point of V-shaped neckline. White cotton-poplin flared trousers, pockets set under waistband, no turn-ups. 5 Cream cotton-muslin beach dress, buttons from hemline to under bust-level, low collarless neckline, short cape sleeves cut in one piece with upper bodice, gathered shaping under bust, fitted bodice from waist to under bust, ground-length flared skirt. Pale-coffee lacquered-straw hat, shallow crown, wide brim. Coffee canvas mules, peep toes, rope platform soles.

Underwear and Negligee

1 Deep-blue synthetic-silk dressing gown patterned with large yellow flowers, wrapover front, self-fabric tie-belt, long shawl collar, full-length inset sleeves, stitched cuffs, hip-level patch pockets. Dark-blue cotton-poplin pyjama trousers. Dark-blue leather slippers. 2 Sky-blue knitted-silk-jersey two-piece pyjama suit patterned with blue-grey herringbone design: long top, buttoned-strap fastening and high round neckline bound in plain navy-blue silk-jersey, matching tie-belt and full-length inset sleeve bindings, large hip-level patch pockets; wide trousers. Navy-blue leather slippers. 3 White knitted-cotton singlet, deep-cut armholes, self-bound and machine top-stitched, matching low scooped neckline. White cotton-poplin boxer shorts, red and yellow pattern, elasticated waistband, front fly opening, short wide legs. 4 Flesh-coloured stretch-nylon bra, wide scooped neckline, unstructured cups, adjustable stretch halter-straps, back fastening. Flesh-coloured briefs, elasticated sides. 5 Pale-mustard-yellow brushed-cotton nightdress, high waist position marked by cream satin belt tied into large bow on centre-front, long flared sleeves cut in one with unfitted bodice and edged in cream lace, matching two rows of lace forming centre-front decorative panel under high round neckline and hem of ankle-length skirt. Yellow satin slippers, embroidered trim.

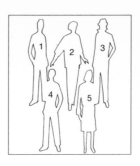
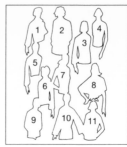

1975 Day Wear

1 Green showerproof cotton-poplin raincoat, single-breasted, wide lapels, epaulettes on dropped shoulderline, full sleeves set into large armholes, narrow cuffs, drawstring waist tied into bow at front, gathered skirts to below knee, shaped welt pockets. Beige blouse, cowl neck. Green silk scarf. Tan felt hat. Tan leather shoes, high straight heels. **2** Blue-grey wool-jersey two-piece suit: collarless jacket, edge-to-edge rouleau loop and self-covered-button fastening under low V-shaped neckline, matching fastening on cuffs of three-quarter-length inset sleeves, shoulder yoke, gathered shaping over bust, flared skirts, rounded edges; flared panelled skirt. Brimless navy-blue felt hat. Navy-blue feather boa. Navy-blue patent-leather bar-strap shoes, scalloped open sides and fronts, high heels. **3** Oatmeal and beige wool-tweed two-piece suit: long jacket, edge-to-edge fastening, three-quarter-length inset sleeves, deep turned-back cuffs, large patch pockets, twisted brown leather belt; straight skirt. Brown wool beret. Brown, oatmeal and beige flecked wool-tweed stole, thick brown wool fringe. Brown leather shoes, ankle straps, cut-away sides, high heels. **4** Tangerine wool two-piece trouser suit: single-breasted fitted jacket, wide lapels, large collar, narrow inset sleeves, patch pockets, top-stitched edges and detail; straight-cut trousers. Light brown wool sweater. Cream silk scarf patterned in tangerine. Brown wool beret. Leather shoes, flat heels. **5** Double-breasted navy-blue wool overcoat, wide lapels, large collar, shoulder epaulettes, button trim, self-fabric buckled belt, matching sleeve trim, hip-level welt pockets in knee-length skirts. Dark-grey flannel trousers, no turn-ups. Pale-grey wool collar-attached shirt. Navy-blue silk scarf. Black leather ankle-boots.

Evening Wear

1 Evening dress, hip-length fitted petticoat bodice, embroidered with shiny black beads and sequins from low neckline to hip seam, narrow black satin rouleau shoulder straps, ankle-length pleated black silk-crepe skirt. Black silk flower worn on right shoulder strap. Black satin shoes, peep toes, high straight heels. **2** Gold panne-velvet evening dress, wide square neckline above shaped yoke, full-length sleeves gathered into armholes and into fitted cuffs, ankle-length skirt gathered from yoke seam. Draped turban to match dress. Gold satin boots, thin platform soles. **3** Ankle-length ice-blue pleated silk evening dress, fitted bodice, high waist seam, low square neckline infilled with embroidered silk, elbow-length cape sleeves falling to hip-level at back, cream satin ribbon trim, matching hems of three-tier skirt. Cream and blue satin flower worn on left shoulder. Cream kid-leather ankle-strap shoes, open sides, high straight heels. **4** Dark-plum satin evening dress, low V-shaped neckline in bra top, high waist seam, low back, floor-length semi-fitted flared skirt edged with wide self-fabric gathered frill. Pale-pink triangular silk shawl, patterned with stylized gold flowers, wide gold-fringed edge. Gold leather strap sandals, thin platform soles. **5** Silver sequined evening dress, fitted bodice, apron front, narrow silver satin rouleau shoulder straps, low back, flared skirt fitted over hips. Silver kid shoes.

Sports and Leisure Wear

1 Ski wear. Two-piece red nylon ski suit: lined and padded jacket, front zip fastening from hemline to under yellow stand collar which matches colour of inset epaulettes, stripe on outer sleeve and buttoned sleeve cuffs, zipped pockets, top-stitched edges and detail; interlined trousers. Red knitted-wool pull-on hat. Red and yellow padded leather gloves. Red ski boots. **2** Country wear. Orange wool-tweed unfitted top, large wing collar, wide three-quarter-length sleeves, hems trimmed with rows of machine top-stitching to match tops of patch pockets. Yellow jersey sweater, draped polo-neck collar, long sleeves, narrow stitched cuffs. Straight-cut dark-yellow wool trousers. Dark-yellow beret. Tan and cream leather lace-up shoes. **3** Golf. Yellow knitted-wool sweater, low V-shaped neckline, full-length raglan sleeves, fawn, cream and light-brown pattern above rib to under chest. Beige wool shirt. Straight-cut cream wool trousers, yellow check, deep turn-ups. Oatmeal and yellow flecked wool-tweed hat, self-fabric band and loops. Leather step-in shoes. **4** Ski wear. Green weatherproof cotton-poplin two-piece ski suit: padded and lined semi-fitted jacket, front zip fastening, navy-blue buttoned waistband, matching stand collar, narrow inset sleeves, navy-blue buttoned cuffs, zipped pockets; straight-cut trousers, machine-top-stitched hems. Navy-blue knitted-wool pull-on hat. Navy-blue ski boots. **5** Golf. Weatherproof cotton-poplin two-piece suit: green semi-fitted top, zip fastening in bust-level strap to under neckline of grown-on hood, drawstring waist, bow on front, angled patch pockets, inset sleeves, buttoned cuffs; navy-blue flared skirt, green centre-front inverted box-pleat. Navy-blue wool tights. Navy-blue leather step-in shoes.

Knitwear

1 Blue and grey mix handknitted wool jacket, front zip fastening from hem to under large collar, wide kimono sleeves gathered into cuffs. Hat with plaited brim and long scarf in matching wool. **2** Green hand-knitted cardigan-jacket, openwork design, wrapover front, long ribbed shawl collar matching tie-belt, hem, cuffs of raglan sleeves and tops of patch pockets. **3** Lilac knitted-wool sleeveless slipover, low square neckline, deep-purple outlines matching armholes and trim above ribbed hem, cable-knit design on main body. **4** Pink hand-knitted cotton tank top, narrow halter straps, stripes of blue and green under neckline and above ribbed hem.
5 Tangerine knitted wool-tweed waistcoat, narrow roll collar, single-breasted fastening, deep rib from hem to under bust. **6** Sleeveless cream handknitted lace-stitch slipover, low scooped neckline and armholes edged with narrow rib, matching hem. **7** Strapless blue handknitted tank top, white stripe trim over bust imitating ruching, fine ribbed body, stitched hem. **8** Coral-pink hand-knitted cotton cape top, square neckline, fine shell edge, matching hem, narrow tie-belt. **9** White machine-knitted wool sweater, polo-neck, unfitted body decorated across chest-level with black and red geometric design matching upper part of inset sleeves, narrow red and black stripes above ribbed cuffs and hem. **10** Red, black, purple and orange patterned machine-knitted collarless cardigan-coat, wrapover front edged in black, matching tie-belt and welt pockets, long flared inset sleeves. Black knitted-wool polo-neck sweater. **11** Brown and tan chevron-striped machine-knitted wool-mixture slipover, wide round neckline and low-cut armholes edged in cream, matching deep welt. Brown machine-knitted polo-neck sweater.

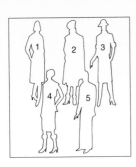
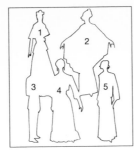
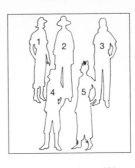

1976 Day Wear

1 Cream wool-jersey dress, bloused bodice, elbow-length cuffed sleeves, top-stitched seam from hem of flared skirt to under boat-shaped neckline, black patent-leather belt, round buckle. Black knitted-cotton polo-neck sweater. Black patent-leather shoes, cut-away sides, round toes, high heels. **2** Three-quarter-length lilac, blue, grey and white flecked wool-tweed sleeveless coat, shoulder-wide collar falling to hemline, large patch pockets on front. Straight skirt in matching fabric, hand-stitched edges and detail. Lightweight grey wool top, low V-shaped neckline, cuffed sleeves, hand-stitched edges and detail, blue suede belt. Blue knitted-cotton sweater, outsized polo-collar, long tight sleeves. Blue wool beret. Blue suede ankle-boots, leather straps, high heels. **3** White cotton dress, bloused bodice, low waist position marked by red leather belt, strap fastening buttoned in red from hem of straight skirt to under stand collar, edges bound in red cotton to match yoke seam and cuff edges on short inset sleeves. Red lacquered-straw hat. Leather shoes, white sling-backs, bar-straps and uppers, red toecaps and high heels. **4** Turquoise knitted-wool two-piece suit: edge-to-edge bolero jacket, loop-and-toggle fastening, blue, green, yellow and red pattern across bustline, edged in red and yellow; semi-fitted dress, polo collar, long tight sleeves, edged in red and yellow, pattern above hemline. Brimless turquoise felt hat. Turquoise suede boots, red fox-fur trim. **5** Single-breasted cream, yellow and grey striped wool jacket, two-button fastening, wide lapels, large patch pockets. Single-breasted collarless grey flannel waistcoat. Matching straight-cut trousers, pleats from waist. Collar-attached yellow cotton shirt. Yellow and grey striped wide silk tie. Yellow and white leather shoes.

Evening Wear

1 Blue, green and turquoise checked silk-taffeta evening dress, off-the-shoulder neckline edged with pleated crystal-blue silk-chiffon, matching deep hip peplum under wide blue satin belt with bow trim, and under wide satin band around hem of full skirt. Blue satin ribbon-bow hair decoration. **2** Fine apricot Terylene-jersey evening dress, fitted bodice and full-length skirt cut in one piece, no waist seam, cape overbodice and sleeves, short over bust, knee-level at sides and back, bare top connected by eight rhinestone straps. Matching strap sandals. **3** Two-piece black wool and mohair evening suit: fitted single-breasted jacket, wide satin lapels, diagonal flap pockets, narrow sleeves; straight-cut trousers, slight flare to hem, no turn-ups, satin trim on outside seam. White cotton collar-attached shirt, large collar, frilled front and cuffs, lace trim. Large black velvet bow-tie. Black suede elastic-sided shoes. **4** Four-piece evening ensemble: ivory silk-chiffon blouse threaded with gold, high round neckline bound and trimmed with gold tissue to match hems of full elbow-length sleeves; voluminous black silk-paper-taffeta skirt, frilled hem under gold and black velvet ribbon trim; short sleeveless quilted black velvet bolero; matching wide cummerbund. Gold tissue turban, twisted crown and wide headband. **5** Silver-grey silk-jersey evening dress, hip-length bloused bodice above top-stitched decoration, low neckline and small keyhole bound with silver and royal-blue striped ribbon braid to match side bodice trim, hems of inset flared sleeves, hem and hip-length side vent of straight skirt. Silver rouleau-loop hair decoration. Silver bar-strap shoes, round toes.

Sports and Leisure Wear

1 Casual wear. Pale-blue brushed-cotton-denim boilersuit, bloused top and trousers cut in one piece, buttoned-strap fastening under lapels faced in red to match cuffs of short sleeves, pointed collar, patch pockets, button trim, trousers rolled to mid-calf-length, self-fabric buckled belt, top-stitched edges and detail. Red and white checked cotton scarf. Denim peaked cap. Red knitted-cotton ankle socks. White leather strap sandals, low heels. **2** Holiday wear. Two-piece pink and white striped polyester and cotton beach suit: edge-to-edge flared collarless jacket, bound front edges, dropped shoulderline, deep cuffs buttoned onto wide sleeves with self-fabric tabs, matching trim on large patch pockets; wide trousers, pleated from buttoned waistband, fly front, pockets set into side seams. Deep-pink knitted-cotton blouse. Pink straw hat. Pink leather sandals. **3** Holiday wear. Blue and green striped cotton shirt, plain blue cotton buttoned-strap fastening and round collar, matching long buttoned epaulettes, top of patch pocket and cuffs of short sleeves, dropped shoulderline, top-stitched edges and detail. Blue cotton-poplin straight-cut trousers, pleated from waistband, self-fabric tie-belt. Blue leather mule sandals. **4** Casual wear. Green polyester and cotton jumpsuit, shirt top and trousers cut in one piece, two patch pockets with pointed flaps, matching pockets on upper part of cuffed sleeves, pointed collar, drawstring waist, fly front, straight-cut trousers. Yellow cowboy boots, scalloped upper edges. **5** Holiday wear. Green cotton-seersucker jumpsuit, shirred bodice under wide self-fabric frill edged in pink to match shoulder straps and bindings at ankle-level on full trousers. Green canvas bar-strap shoes, rope soles, low wedge heels.

Underwear and Negligee

1 Flesh-coloured Lycra moulded bra, narrow shoulder straps, back fastening. Cream rayon knickers, gathers from elasticated waist, wide legs trimmed with nylon lace. **2** Turquoise nylon camiknickers, fitted bra top, cream nylon lace trim, narrow adjustable shoulder straps, fitted body, hems of flared legs trimmed with cream nylon lace. **3** Two-piece silk lounging pyjamas: oyster silk-satin hip-length top patterned with large gold-yellow flowers and leaves, three-quarter-length kimono sleeves, scalloped lace-trimmed hems, matching slashed neckline and hem, plain gold silk-satin tie-belt; wide trousers in matching fabric. Gold satin slippers, peep toes. **4** Pale-peach silk collarless negligee, edge-to-edge, wide pale-cream trim to above frilled hem, self-fabric bow tie at bust-level, three-quarter-length flared sleeves split to elbow, lace trim. Cream satin house slippers, peep toes. **5** Two-piece sky-blue rayon pyjama suit: single-breasted collarless jacket, deep-blue rayon-satin strap fastening continuing around neck, piped in white to match cuffs of elbow-length inset sleeves, deep-blue rayon satin-covered buttons, curved seam with shaping under bust; flared trousers matching jacket, wide hems bound in white. Flat blue satin pumps, bow trim.

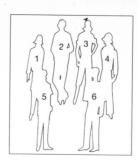
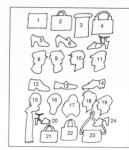

1977 Day Wear

1 Two-piece grey and white striped wool and mohair suit: single-breasted jacket, wide lapels, padded shoulders; straight-cut trousers, turn-ups, pleats from deep waistband, red leather belt. Pale-grey silk collar-attached shirt. White and red spotted silk bow-tie. Red leather step-in shoes, round toes, flat heels. White silk socks. **2** Beige suede hooded coat, sheepskin lining and cuffs, single-breasted wooden toggle fastening, flared inset sleeves, black, orange and yellow machine-embroidered decoration matching hem of flared skirts, self-fabric tie-belt, piped hip-level pockets. Black leather gloves and boots, round toes, high heels. **3** Sage-green brushed-cotton three-piece ensemble with all-over pattern of multicoloured flowers: quilted sleeveless waistcoat, single-breasted fastening under round neckline, self-fabric covered buttons, piped edges, pleated hem, black braid trim; blouse, pleated neckline, black shoestring bow tie, full sleeves gathered into buttoned cuffs, pleated hems; full gathered skirt, deep gathered frill on hem. Long black leather boots, round toes. **4** Mid-calf-width dark-rust-brown overcoat, wrapover fastening with wide self-fabric tie-belt, wide lapels, large collar worn turned up, narrow yoke, inset sleeves, hip-level welt pockets, top-stitched edges and detail. Straight-cut grey flannel trousers, no turn-ups. Light-grey wool collar-attached shirt. Petrol-blue wool tie. Oxblood-red step-in shoes. **5** Fine rayon-jersey dress, dark-green yoke spotted in white and navy-blue, short T-shirt sleeves, padded shoulders, round neckline, hip yoke in matching colours, white bloused bodice spotted in dark-green and navy-blue, drawstring waist, knee-length skirt from hip-level in colours to match bodice. Navy-blue sling-back strap sandals, peep toes, high slender heels.

Wedding Wear

1 Ivory silk wedding dress, fitted lace bodice, high waist marked by scalloped edge, matching high stand collar, deep cuffs of long gathered sleeves and border above gathered frill on ground-length flared skirt. Headdress of tiny silk roses and lily of the valley. **2** Cream silk two-piece Victorian-style wedding suit: fitted single-breasted jacket, fastening with tiny buttons from waist-level to under large collar, self-fabric piping and frilled edge, matching front opening, edge of peplum and hems of long inset sleeves, large cream satin bow on centre-back waist, two small bows on waist either side centre-front; ankle-length flared skirt, deep scallops of pleated silk at mid-calf-level topped with satin bows, hem edged in silk pleating. Small cream silk hat, large bow trim, silk-tulle veil. Cream satin shoes, bow trim. **3** Pale-turquoise silk-chiffon wedding dress patterned with cream leaves, sleeveless fitted bodice, high stand collar, bias-cut cape set into side panel front and back covering arms to elbow and dipping to knee-level at front and mid-calf at back. Pale-turquoise transparent-nylon hat decorated with rows of machine top-stitching, wide brim, cream and turquoise silk flower trim. **4** Mid-calf-length white cotton wedding dress, low square neckline, edged pintucked band, self-fabric binding, lace trim and lace edging, matching bodice side panel seams, frilled cuffs of three-quarter-length full sleeves and edges of three-tier gathered skirt, wide cummerbund. Headdress of fresh flowers. White suede boots. **5** Ground-length white nylon wedding dress, fitted bodice, transparent yoke embroidered with pearl and crystal beads to match high stand collar and cuffs of gathered transparent sleeves, full skirt, long train, hem edged with pearl and crystal beads. Small spray of silk flowers on back of head, long silk-tulle veil.

Sports and Leisure Wear

1 Country wear. Two-piece lilac, blue and grey herringbone wool-tweed suit: knee-length semi-fitted dress, buttoned-strap fastening, shirt collar, cuffed shirt sleeves, flared skirt; narrow trousers. Lilac polo-neck sweater. Purple wool scarf, fringed hems. Purple leather ankle-boots. **2** Country wear. Rust and brown wool-tweed casual jacket, press-stud fastening, shirt collar, raglan sleeves, knitted cuffs, matching side hip-band, diagonal pockets, strap-and-stud trim. Brown needlecord trousers. Rust wool scarf. Brown leather elastic-sided ankle-boots. **3** Casual wear. Orange cotton jumpsuit, front zip fastening, shirt collar, semi-fitted top and trousers cut in one piece without waist seam, short cuffed sleeves, strap-and-button trim, matching epaulettes, two patch pockets, buttoned flaps, matching diagonally-set pockets. Orange and cream leather cowboy boots. **4** Golf. Two-piece beige wool trouser suit flecked in orange, brown and black: short jacket, front zip fastening, shirt collar, cuffed shirt sleeves, vertical welt pockets set into side panel seams, hipband with strap-and-button trim; flared trousers. Beige wool polo-neck sweater. Brown and cream wool-tweed hat. Cream and orange leather step-in shoes, fringed tongues. **5** Country wear. Black and red wool top; horizontally-striped scarf collar, buttoned-strap fastening and deep cuffs; sleeves and body in small check; piped pockets. Black stretch-wool trousers. Black leather elastic-sided ankle-boots. **6** Golf. Ochre knitted-wool cardigan-jacket, front zip fastening edged with panels of brown suede, matching side panel seams, welt pockets and shirt collar, inset sleeves, ribbed cuffs and hipband. Ochre knitted-wool polo-neck sweater. Light-brown, ochre and brown checked wool flared trousers. Brown wool peaked cap. Leather step-in shoes, fringed tongues.

Accessories

1 Maroon leather clutch bag, edged and trimmed in black suede. **2** Unstructured black leather handbag, double padded rouleau handles. **3** Tan leather bag, flap-and-clasp fastening, front pocket, short handle. **4** Green leather bag, double padded rouleau handles, front pocket with flap. **5** Navy-blue and white leather lace-up brogues, high straight heels. **6** Grey leather shoes, high fringed tongues, high straight heels. **7** Red leather sling-back shoes, ankle straps, high straight heels. **8** Brown cotton-corduroy peaked cap. **9** Blue denim peaked cap, top-stitched sectioned crown, button trim. **10** Orange, cream and brown checked wool peaked cap, button trim. **11** Olive-green waterproof-cotton peaked golfer's cap. **12** Beige suede lace-up ankle-boots, man-made soles and heels. **13** Black leather step-in shoes, high tongues, stitched fronts, stacked heels. **14** Red and cream leather lace-up golf shoes, laces tied through turned-down fringed tongues, spiked soles and heels. **15** Red wool-jersey hat, narrow turned-down top-stitched brim, small fitted crown, twisted padded self-fabric roll band. Long red wool scarf, fringed hems. **16** Sage-green wool beret, brooch trim. **17** Black sequined brimless evening cap. **18** Brimless red fox-fur hat. **19** Cream felt hat, narrow turned-down brim, rounded crown, double self-fabric bands. **20** Navy-blue leather sling-back shoes, peep toes, ankle straps, high straight heels. **21** Light-brown baby-snakeskin handbag, double handle, zip fastening. **22** Tan leather handbag, double handles through rings, top-stitched curved panel seam, zip fastening. **23** Light-brown canvas shoulder bag, long brown leather handle, matching trim. **24** Pale-blue denim mules, peep toes, cut-out flower motifs, wooden platform soles and high straight heels.

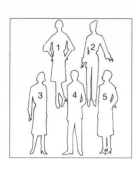

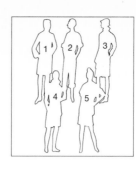
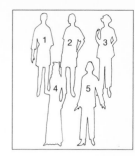

1978 Day Wear

1 Dusty-pink Tricel-jersey dress, high round neckline, centre-front split, shoulder yoke and narrow front panel cut in one piece, bloused bodice, sleeves gathered under shoulder pads and into buttoned cuffs on elbow, skirt gathered from shaped hip yoke, self-fabric tie-belt, top-stitched edges and detail. Cream leather T-strap shoes, pointed toes, high shaped heels. **2** Two-piece oatmeal wool trouser suit: wrapover jacket, long roll collar, fastened with self-fabric tie-belt, large hip-level patch pockets, gathered shaping from under narrow shoulder yoke, long wide inset sleeves, deep cuffs, shoulder pads, top-stitched edges and detail; narrow trousers. Cream silk blouse, stand collar, long sleeves. Cream suede ankle-boots, elongated square toes. **3** Grey flannel dress, semi-fitted bodice, buttoned-strap fastening to under bound round neckline, long raglan sleeves cut in one with pintucked cuffs, matching tucks on shoulderline above pads, self-fabric buckled belt, flared skirt, top-stitched edges and detail. Black leather shoes, white trim, peep toes, high shaped heels. **4** Two-piece cream silk-and-wool-mixture tweed suit: double-breasted shaped jacket, narrow lapels, large patch pockets; straight-cut trousers, no turn-ups. Cream silk collar-attached shirt. Cream silk tie. Light-beige suede lace-up shoes, top-stitched trim. **5** Grey-green wool wrapover coat, fastened with self-fabric buckled belt worn knotted at front, outsized collar, wide sleeves cut in one piece with floating yoke, belt trim above wrists, large hip-level patch pockets, flared skirts, top-stitched edges and detail. White wool sweater, outsized polo-neck collar. Matching pull-on hat. Knee-high dark-green leather unfitted boots, high heels, pointed toes.

Evening Wear

1 Salmon-pink silk-taffeta evening dress, fitted bodice, low square neckline, elbow-length circular-cut cap sleeves gathered into armholes over small shoulder pads, two-tier skirt, knee-length top tier gathered from high waist position, ankle-length underskirt. Gold kid strap sandals. **2** Midnight-blue silk-jersey evening dress, embroidered all over with crystal beads in various sizes, fitted bodice and ankle-length straight skirt cut in one piece without waist seam, navy-blue silk-jersey shoulder yoke, shallow stand collar and cuffs of long inset sleeves embroidered to match dress, padded shoulders. Silver kid strap sandals. **3** Blue-grey wool-crepe evening dress, wrist-length asymmetric shoulder cape gathered into brooch on one shoulder, lined in fuchsia-pink silk, ankle-length straight skirt lined to match, split from hem to hip-level. Fuchsia-pink satin T-strap sandals. **4** Two-piece royal-blue Tricel-jersey evening pants suit: long unfitted top, gathered from under off-the-shoulder frilled collar, long full sleeves gathered into armholes, elasticated on wrist; matching full harem pants elasticated on ankles. Silver kid strap sandals, high slender heels. **5** Three-piece evening ensemble: black velvet fitted strapless bodice; ankle-length black silk-jersey drainpipe trousers, black satin waistband, bow trim; wrist-length circular-cut black silk-chiffon shoulder cape, black satin stand collar, back opening, matching bound hem. Black satin strap sandals, high slender heels.

Sports and Leisure Wear

1 Sailing. Midnight-blue waterproof cotton-poplin bloused top, hood set into V-shaped neckline, self-fabric infill, long raglan sleeves elasticated at wrist, drawstring waist, top-stitched edges and detail. White cotton-sailcloth shorts, pleated from waist, fly front, pockets set into side seams. White canvas lace-up shoes, rubber soles and heels. **2** Sailing/Holiday wear. Red and white vertically-striped bloused top, shirt collar set into V-shaped neckline, self-fabric infill with horizontal stripes matching deep cuffs of wide elbow-length raglan sleeves. White cotton-poplin trousers, drawstring waist, large patch pockets at each side hip, straight-cut legs worn rolled to mid-calf-level. Red canvas T-strap shoes, openwork decoration on fronts, high wedge heels covered in rope. **3** Holiday wear. Collarless single-breasted orange wool waistcoat, deep armholes, small shaped flap pockets, button trim, top-stitched edges and detail; flared shorts in matching fabric, large patch pockets either side below hip-level, shaped flaps, button trim, pleated from deep waistband, green leather buckled belt. Yellow cotton blouse, shirt sleeves, button cuffs, collar worn open and turned up. Green cotton hat, sectioned crown, button trim, narrow brim turned down. Yellow cotton ankle socks. Green leather lace-up shoes, flat heels. **4** Beach wear. Blue and white checked cotton shirt worn open, shirt collar worn turned up, short inset sleeves, deep cuffs. Red and white knitted-cotton T-shirt, round neckline and hem bound in white. White cotton shorts, fly front, pockets set in side seams. Red leather T-strap sandals. **5** Beachwear. Outsized yellow knitted-cotton T-shirt-dress, wide round neckline, wide short sleeves cut in one with hip-length bloused bodice and mini-length skirt, split from hem to hip either side, top-stitched edges.

Negligee

1 Short bright-yellow cotton-towelling bathrobe, collarless wrapover front, wide self-fabric binding matching hems of three-quarter-length kimono sleeves, self-fabric tie-belt, large hip-length patch pockets. **2** Two-piece pale-blue cotton pyjama suit: single-breasted collarless jacket, press-stud fastening, wide self-fabric binding, short inset sleeves, single chest-level patch pocket; wide shorts, fly fastening, drawstring waist. Cream leather mule slippers, toolwork design on fronts. **3** Two-piece pink cotton pyjama suit: hip-length sleeveless top, stand collar embroidered with multicoloured flowers and leaves, matching wrapover bib front, self-fabric rouleau-bow fastening, gathers from under bust; mid-calf-length trousers. Pink velvet mule slippers, feather trim. **4** Fine white silk nightdress, wrapover front secured on hip with satin ribbons tied into large bow, low neckline, edges and hem trimmed with wide border of lace, double white satin rouleau straps, low back. White satin slippers, pointed toes, bow trim. **5** Two-piece pale-peach-pink satin pyjama suit patterned with peach-pink and white sprays of flowers: hip-length semi-fitted jacket, single-breasted buttoned-strap fastening from hem to under shaped stand collar, inset sleeves flare to wrists, hems bound in self-fabric to match hem of jacket, side split, hems of straight-cut ankle-length trousers and side splits on side seams. Cream silk mule slippers, peep toes, medium-high heels.

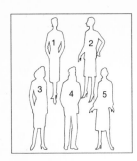

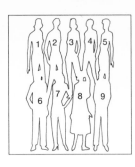
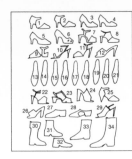

1979 Day Wear

1 Cream knitted-cotton dress patterned with pale-blue broken stripes, fitted bodice, slashed neckline, padded shoulders, three-quarter-length sleeves, plain pale-blue knitted-cotton cuffs, matching hip-level welt pockets in knee-length straight skirt, wide pale-blue leather belt. Cream leather shoes, pointed toes, dark-blue toecaps, heel trim and high spike heels. 2 Navy-blue linen double-breasted tailored jacket, narrow lapels, long inset sleeves, button trim, padded shoulders, wide stitched canvas and leather belt. Knee-length pale-grey linen wrapover skirt, spotted in pink. Navy-blue silk-jersey crownless turban. Navy-blue leather strap sandals, high spike heels. 3 Mint-green Tricel-jersey two-piece suit: collarless edge-to-edge jacket, loop-and-button fastening from waist to under low V-shaped neckline, bloused bodice, shaping gathers under narrow shoulder yoke, padded shoulders, narrow inset sleeves, draped cummerbund, hip-level skirts with rounded edges; narrow knee-length skirt. Dark-beige leather shoes, peep toes, high spike heels. 4 Burgundy wool-tweed single-breasted jacket, shirt-style collar worn turned up, patch pockets, buttoned shaped flaps, top-stitched edges and detail. Narrow dark-grey heavy-cotton trousers, pleated from waist, no turn-ups. Grey cotton-tweed collar-attached shirt. Grey and burgundy hand-knitted sweater, low V-shaped neckline. Grey cotton peaked cap. Dark-grey leather shoes, strap-and-buckle fastening, square toes. 5 Pale-blue silk-jersey dress, full bodice and skirt cut in one piece, gathered from narrow shoulder yoke, padded shoulders, full inset sleeves gathered into cuffs, dress buttons through from hem to under narrow peter-pan collar worn turned up. Pale-blue leather shoes, pointed toes, high spike heels.

Evening Wear

1 Blue-grey silk-taffeta strapless evening dress, fitted and boned bodice, edges and wrapover effect bound and frilled in cream silk-taffeta to match edges and hems of two-tier gathered skirts and hem of large bow on side hip, trimmed with large cream silk flowers. 2 White silk-chiffon full-length dinner dress, bloused bodice gathered from above wide belt, black bead embroidery matching narrow shoulder yoke and upper sleeve trim, gathered shaping over bust, ground-length full gathered skirt. 3 Two-piece black striped wool-and-silk-mixture evening suit: double-breasted jacket, narrow satin-faced roll collar, matching covered buttons, three patch pockets, square shoulders; narrow trousers, satin braid trim on outside seams, no turn-ups. White silk shirt, attached collar, round edges. Black satin bow-tie. Black patent-leather step-in shoes. 4 Primrose-yellow Tricel-jersey sleeveless evening dress, bloused bodice draped from padded shoulders to triangular inset panel on front under low V-shaped neckline, wide self-fabric belt, ground-length straight skirt, draped front panel. Gold kid shoes. 5 Two-piece black silk dinner ensemble, fabric decorated with wide-spaced rows of vertical pintucks: hip-length top, self-fabric belt tied into bow on side, hem edged and trimmed with lace and bands of fine pintucks to match yoke under slashed neckline, hems of long flared inset sleeves and hem of knee-length gathered skirt. Black silk flower worn on one shoulder. Black patent-leather shoes, pointed toes, high spike heels.

Sports and Leisure Wear

1 Swimwear. White Lycra swimsuit with outsized yellow and orange flower pattern, V-plunge neckline, halter fastening at back, covered button trim on centre-front seam, low back. 2 Swimwear. Mauve Lycra swimsuit, low V-shaped neckline to waist-level, ruched detail, halter fastening at back, low back. 3 Swimwear. Cerise, pink and blue striped and spotted Lycra swimsuit, tab front, threaded rouleau halter strap, back fastening, scooped back. 4 Swimwear. Green nylon and cotton swimsuit, keyhole under scooped neckline, narrow halter straps, back fastening, scooped back. 5 Swimwear. Backless Lycra swimsuit, deep V-shaped neckline incorporating wide halter straps from top of bikini briefs, back fastening, restraining rouleau strap under bust to back. 6 Exercise wear. Two-piece pink knitted-cotton tracksuit: bloused top, V-shaped neckline bound in red, drawstring waist matches hems of sleeves and trousers, bound pockets. Crownless pink plastic visor. Pink and red canvas trainers. 7 Holiday/Casual wear. Shiny silver-blue stretch-Lycra top, low scooped neckline, narrow shoulder straps. Blue Tricel-jersey trousers, gathered from waist to narrow hems, hip-level pockets. Blue suede belt, self-fabric buckle. Blue suede mules, peep toes, wooden soles and high heels. 8 Beachwear. Knee-length green cotton dress with black and white leaf pattern, gathered from bound scooped neckline, rouleau straps tied into bows on shoulders. White plastic mules, peep toes, cork soles and wedge heels. 9 Exercise wear. Two-piece red knitted-cotton tracksuit: unfitted top, front zip fastening from hem to under navy-blue stand collar which matches sleeve cuffs and trim on sleeve head; unfitted trousers, fly fastening, navy-blue cuffs on ankles. Red and navy canvas and leather trainers.

Footwear

1 Beige leather shoes, tan leather bar-straps, toecaps, heels and trim. 2 Grey leather shoes, green leather bar-straps, heels and trim. 3 White leather shoes, navy-blue toecaps and heels. 4 Black patent-leather shoes, grey leather trim. 5 Brown leather shoes, black leather heels and trim. 6 Red leather shoes, strap fronts. 7 Sling-back cream leather bar-strap sandals, peep toes. 8 Sling-back green leather T-strap sandals. 9 Cream leather sling-back shoes, low wedge heels, fronts banded in brown, peep toes. 10 Pearlized-blue leather sling-back sandals, tied ankle straps. 11 Beige leather sling-back shoes, ankle straps, black leather trim, peep toes. 12 Tan leather mules, peep toes, wooden soles and heels. 13 Brown leather step-in shoes, tasselled tie-trim. 14 White canvas lace-up shoes, brown leather soles and heels. 15 Brown suede lace-up ankle-boots, toecaps. 16 Red leather perforated shoes. 17 Tan suede shoes, cross-strap-and-buckle fastening. 18 Brown leather shoes, narrow cross-strap fastening. 19 Brown suede step-in perforated shoes. 20 Green leather step-in shoes. 21 Yellow leather lace-up shoes, hand-stitched trim. 22 Gold kid sling-back sandals, ankle straps, peep toes. 23 Sling-back blue leather T-strap sandals. 24. Tan leather perforated mules, crossed straps. 25 Blue suede shoes, scalloped edges, ankle straps, conical heels. 26 Mules, wooden soles, leather strap fronts. 27 Pink suede lace-up shoes, rubber soles and heels. 28 Orange leather T-strap sandals. 29 Gold kid rouleau-strap sandals, spike heels. 30 Green boots, top-stitched cuffs. 31 Brown leather lace-up ankle-boots, light-brown canvas sides. 32 Brown leather lace-up boots. 33 Tan leather boots, beige canvas uppers, vertical top-stitching. 34 Green leather lace-up boots.

Chart of the Development of 1970s Fashion

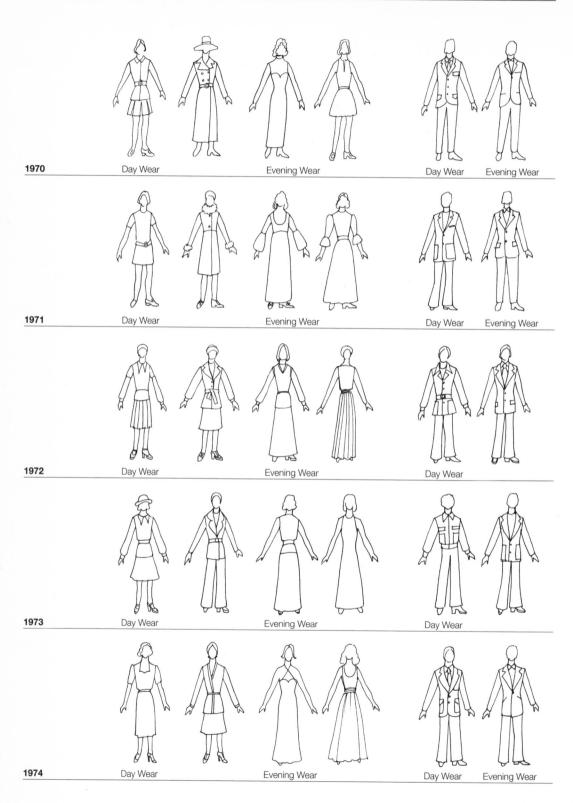

1970   Day Wear   Evening Wear   Day Wear   Evening Wear

1971   Day Wear   Evening Wear   Day Wear   Evening Wear

1972   Day Wear   Evening Wear   Day Wear

1973   Day Wear   Evening Wear   Day Wear

1974   Day Wear   Evening Wear   Day Wear   Evening Wear

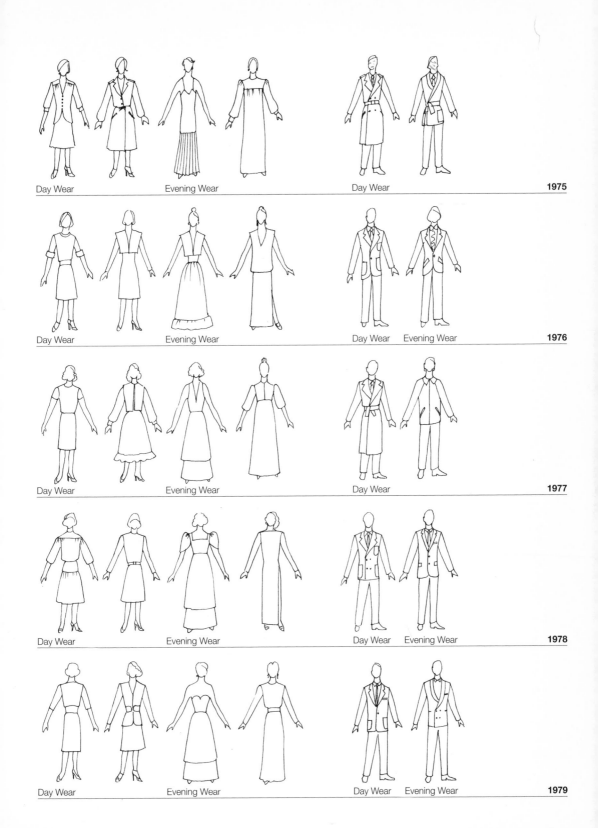

Day Wear   Evening Wear   Day Wear   **1975**

Day Wear   Evening Wear   Day Wear   Evening Wear   **1976**

Day Wear   Evening Wear   Day Wear   **1977**

Day Wear   Evening Wear   Day Wear   Evening Wear   **1978**

Day Wear   Evening Wear   Day Wear   Evening Wear   **1979**

Biographies of Designers

Armani, Giorgio 1935–.
Designer. Born Piacenza, Italy.
Worked from 1954 to 1960 as a
window stylist, and eventually as
fashion coordinator, for the Italian
department store La Rinascente.
From 1960 to 1970 he designed
menswear for Cerruti, and from
1970 to 1974 worked freelance
for Ungaro, among others.
Opened his own company in
1975. Creates unstructured,
though precisely tailored clothing
from fine materials. He was
hugely influential during the late
1970s and 1980s with his broad-
shouldered, pared-down suits
for men and his women's clothes
based on masculine garments.

Bates, John 1938–. Designer.
Born Ponteland, England. Started
the company Jean Varon in the
early 1960s and soon became
known as one of that decade's
most audacious designers,
producing the briefest of mini-
skirts, trouser suits, catsuits and
broderie-anglaise eveningwear.
Among his most widely copied
designs were the costumes he
created for the actress Diana
Rigg in the British TV series *The
Avengers*. During the 1970s his
style became more sophisticated
and he had particular success
with his extra-long maxi coats
and fluid evening dresses.

Beene, Geoffrey 1927–.
Designer. Born Haynesville,
Louisiana, USA. Studied at the
Traphagen School of Fashion,
New York. In the late 1940s
moved to Paris where he trained
at the Académie Julian and at
Molyneux. On his return to New
York in 1948, he worked for
a number of ready-to-wear
companies before founding
his own firm in 1963. Designs
graphically striking garments
which combine couture quality
with the ease of modern
sportswear. Has shown originality
in mixing fabrics and in the use
of synthetic materials.

Blass, Bill (William Ralph)
1922–2002. Designer. Born Fort
Wayne, Indiana, USA. After World
War II joined Anne Miller & Co.
who merged with Maurice
Rentner Ltd in 1959. He became
vice president in 1962 and from
1970 the company went under
his own name. Though he often
borrowed from the male wardrobe
for his sportswear, Blass tailored
his suits with a curved silhouette
which flattered the female shape.
He was known for his extravagant
use of ruffles and lace.

Bohan, Marc 1926–. Born Paris,
France. Worked freelance for
Piguet, Molyneux and Patou,
among others before he was
appointed director of Dior's
English operations in London
in 1958. In 1961 he succeeded
Saint Laurent as head designer
in Paris. He quickly established
a reputation for maintaining the
refined, romantic image of Dior
while adapting popular, youthful
styles to haute couture. He is
known for his elegant evening
gowns in rich fabrics.

Burrows, Stephen (Gerald)
1943–. Designer. Born Newark,
New Jersey, USA. Studied at
Philadelphia Museum College of
Art and the Fashion Institute of
Technology in New York before
opening a boutique in 1968.
Founded his own firm in 1973.
Became famous for clinging,
glitzy clothes including highly
popular designs such as slinky
jersey dresses in bright colours
and layered chiffon tops and
skirts. Many of Burrows's
garments are recognizable by
his use of machine-made
stitching to produce a crinkled
'lettuce' effect on hemlines.

Cardin, Pierre 1922–. Designer.
Born San Biago di Callalta, near
Venice, Italy, to French parents.
Worked for a tailor in Vichy from
the age of seventeen. Moved to
Paris in 1944 and found work
with Paquin, Schiaparelli and
Dior. In 1947 designed the
costumes for Jean Cocteau's
film *La Belle et la bête* and over
the following years established
a reputation as a theatrical
costumier. Opened his own
house in 1950. By the 1960s he
had developed into an original
and influential designer for both
men and women. In 1964 he
showed his avant-garde 'Space
Age' collection and became
famous for his catsuits, mini-
skirts and bodystockings. In
the 1970s he continued to
show innovative designs using
more supple fabrics, often with
sunray pleating; he also won
acclaim for his layered chiffon
eveningwear.

Clark, Ossie 1942–96. Designer.
Born Liverpool, England. From
1957 to 1961 attended
Manchester College of Art and
the Royal College of Art in
London. Began designing for the
boutique Quorum while still a
student and became a full-time
designer in 1966. Responsible
for some of the most innovative

styles of the 1960s and 1970s,
including hot-pants, maxi coats,
gypsy-style dresses and short,
zipped leather motorcycle jackets
with large collars. During the
1970s he was known for long,
wraparound dresses, often with
deep necklines and small waists.

de la Renta, Oscar 1932–.
Designer. Born Santo Domingo,
Dominican Republic. Studied at
the Academia de San Fernando.
His first design, for a debutante
gown for the daughter of the
US ambassador to Spain, was
featured on the cover of *Life* and
led to a job with Balenciaga. In
1961 he was made assistant to
Castillo at Lanvin in Paris and
moved with Castillo to Elizabeth
Arden in New York in 1963. In
1965, he began working for Jane
Derby but on her retirement in
the same year he founded his
own house. Best known for his
dramatic evening wear, often
extravagantly trimmed. During
the 1970s he won acclaim for
peasant-style garments.

Galanos, James 1924–.
Designer. Born Philadelphia,
USA. Galanos was apprenticed
to Piguet in Paris in 1947, and in
1951 founded his own house,
based in Los Angeles. His first
show in 1953 brought immediate
success. He is known for his high
standards of tailoring and cutting
and for his use of luxurious
fabrics. During the 1960s and
1970s he designed many close-
fitting, classically draped evening
dresses, often with large sleeves
and low-cut backs.

Gaultier, Jean-Paul 1952–.
Born Paris, France. At the age
of seventeen he sent sketches
to several couture houses and
was invited to work for Cardin for
one year. He then designed for
Jacques Esterel and Jean Patou,
among others. In 1977 he set up
his own company, producing
witty, anarchic fashions which
fused Parisian glamour with
fleamarket kitsch and London
streetstyles. He has developed
a reputation as an innovative
designer whose work challenges
accepted boundaries of gender.

Gibb, Bill 1943–88. Born
Fraserburgh, Scotland. Studied in
London at St Martin's School of
Art and the Royal College of Art
before joining Baccarat. In 1970
he was named 'Designer of the
Year' by British *Vogue* and in
1971 established his own
company. Became known for his

lavish, romantic eveningwear,
achieving particular success with
diaphanous chiffon dresses and
embroidered and appliquéd
jersey dresses.

**Givenchy, Hubert (James
Marcel Taffin) de** 1927–.
Designer. Born Beauvais, France.
Worked for Fath, Piguet, Lelong
and Schiaparelli before opening
his own business in 1952. During
the 1950s his young, playful style
became more sombre under the
influence of Balenciaga. Givenchy
was hugely influential, particularly
through his designs for Audrey
Hepburn in the 1961 film
Breakfast at Tiffany's. In the
1970s he continued to produce
chic, wearable couture.

Halston, Roy 1932–90.
Designer. Born Des Moines,
Iowa, USA. Opened a millinery
salon in 1953 in Chicago before
moving to New York in 1958 to
work for the milliner Lilly Daché
and then for Bergdorf Goodman.
Set up his own ready-to-wear
firm in 1966, gaining a reputation
for sexy, glamorous clothes with a
slim silhouette. He was one of the
most sophisticated and influential
designers of the 1970s. Among
his most widely copied designs
were his ultrasuede shirtwaist
dress of 1972 and his bias-cut
evening dresses with one
shoulder strap.

Kamali, Norma 1945–.
Designer. Born New York, USA.
Studied fashion illustration at the
Fashion Institute of Technology in
New York. Between 1967 and
1978 worked as a freelance
designer, opening a boutique with
her husband in 1968. In the
1970s produced extrovert, body-
conscious clothes such as hot
pants and gold lamé maillots
inspired by streetstyles. By 1978,
when she set up the company
OMO (On My Own), she was
recognized as one of the most
innovative designers of the
decade. Introduced sweatshirting
for daywear in the late 1970s.

Kenzo 1939–. Designer. Born
Kenzo Takada in Kyoto, Japan.
Attended the Bunka Gakuin
College of Fashion in Tokyo.
Moved to Paris in 1964 and sold
his designs to Feraud, Rodier
and others. In 1970 opened his
Jungle Jap boutique in Paris and
achieved immediate success with
casual, exuberant designs often
made in cotton. Based many
of his garments on Japanese
traditions of layering fabric

around the body. Finds inspiration in ethnic costumes which he mixes and reinterprets to produce colourful, trendsetting garments. Also known for mixing prints and experimenting with texture.

Klein, Calvin (Richard) 1942–. Designer. Born New York, USA. After studying at the New York Fashion Institute of Technology, Klein joined Dan Millstein in 1962 and then worked freelance until 1968 when he set up Calvin Klein Co. Became famous for his sleek, understated suits and sportswear made from natural fabrics. By the late 1970s his designs had become increasingly sophisticated, with broad-shouldered jackets and slim, softly tailored separates. Known for the hugely successful marketing of his 'designer label' jeans and underwear.

Lagerfeld, Karl (Otto) 1938–. Designer. Born Hamburg, Germany. At the age of seventeen, won first prize for a design for a coat in a competition sponsored by the International Wool Secretariat and was taken on by Balmain. In 1958 he was made art director at Patou. One year later he began working freelance for several design houses, including Chloé, Krizia and Fendi, making a considerable impact on 1970s fashions. His innovations at Fendi included removing the heavy linings in fur coats to make more supple garments and dyeing furs in strong colours. At the ready-to-wear company Chloé he created luxurious, feminine eveningwear of the highest quality. In 1983 he became design director of Chanel and was highly successful with his controversial mixing of Chanel's hallmark tweed suits, gilt buttons and chains with modern, streetstyle elements.

Lauren, Ralph 1939–. Designer. Born New York, USA. While studying business at City College in New York, Lauren worked for Bloomingdale's, Brooks Brothers and others. Appointed designer for Beau Brummell Neckwear in 1967, he created 'Polo', a line of luxury handmade ties. In 1968 he began designing menswear for the Polo division. Womenswear was added in 1971. In 1972 he launched his own label which became associated with classic, Ivy League-style garments. His 'Prairie' look of 1978, based on fringed leather jackets, full-sleeved cotton blouses and

denim skirts worn over white petticoats, was also highly successful. His costumes for Robert Redford in the 1974 film *The Great Gatsby* and his designs for Diane Keaton in *Annie Hall* (1977), were two of the most recognizable styles of the 1970s.

Missoni, Ottavio and Rosita Knitwear designers. Ottavio born 1921 in Dalmatia; Rosita born 1931 in Lombardy, Italy. After founding the Missoni company in 1953, the couple produced their first knitwear collection for Rinascente Stores in 1954 and launched their own label in 1958. They rose to prominence in the 1970s, producing fluid, boldly patterned dresses, coats and sweaters which restored the fashion world's interest in knitwear. Missoni is known for sophisticated knitting techniques and an artistic blending of colour.

Miyake, Issey 1935–. Born Hiroshima, Japan. Graduated in 1964 from Tama University, Tokyo. In 1965 moved to Paris to study at the École de la Chambre Syndicale de la Haute Couture. Then worked for Laroche and Givenchy before joining Geoffrey Beene in New York in 1969. Since his first collection in New York in 1971, he has created highly original garments, many of which can be draped around the body in different ways. Using traditional Japanese techniques of layering fabric, he explores texture and structure with unusual materials such as moulded plastic and woven bamboo. His sculptural designs are timeless.

Montana, Claude 1949–. Designer. Born Paris, France. Began his career by selling handmade papier-mâché jewelry decorated with rhinestones in London street-markets. His designs appeared in British *Vogue* and when he returned to Paris in 1972 he worked for MacDouglas and Complice. Founded his own house in 1979. Produces tough, masculine garments often in leather. In the 1970s his designs strongly influenced French ready-to-wear.

Mugler, Thierry 1948–. Born Strasbourg, France. Joined Gudule boutique in Paris in 1966 as assistant designer. In 1973 he created a collection under the label 'Café de Paris'. Set up his own house in 1974. Strongly influenced by Hollywood glamour

and gangster style, he produces clinging, theatrical clothes which can either be highly minimalist or vampy and ornate. In 1977 was one of the first designers to use padded shoulders, heralding a new shape for the 1980s.

Muir, Jean 1933–95. Designer. Born London, England. After working at Liberty, where she eventually became a sketcher, she joined Jaeger in 1956 and in 1962 began designing a line called Jane & Jane. In 1966 she set up her own company. Known for fluid, refined, timeless clothes in jersey and suede.

Rhodes, Zandra 1940–. Designer. Born Chatham, Kent, England. In 1961 she attended the Royal College of Art in London. First sold her garments from her shop in London. Founded her own house in 1968. Taking her handprinted fabrics as the starting point for her designs, she became famous during the 1970s for fantastic, floating dresses in silk and chiffon, often with handkerchief hems. Her designs feature Art Deco motifs, zigzags and pale, delicate colours. In the late 1970s she revived the crinoline and in 1977 her 'Conceptual Chic' collection brought glamour to Punk styles with garments made from ripped jersey held together with diamanté safety pins.

Rykiel, Sonia 1930–. Designer. Born Paris, France. Began her career by making maternity dresses for herself in 1962. Then designed for her husband's firm 'Laura' and in 1968 set up her own boutique in Galeries Lafayette in Paris. Helped to revive interest in knitwear by creating subtle outfits from soft wools such as angora. Her clinging sweaters, teamed with versatile skirts and trousers, are shaped to suit a slim figure.

Saint Laurent, Yves (Henri Donat Mathieu) 1936–. Designer. Born Oran, Algeria. Won first prize for a design for a cocktail dress in a competition held by the International Wool Secretariat in 1954. In 1955 began working for Dior, taking over the house at the age of twenty-one when Dior died. Though hugely popular, his youthful style did not please Dior's more conventional clientele – he was replaced by Marc Bohan in 1961. Following the establishment of his own house

in the same year, he produced a series of innovative, sophisticated designs including his influential 'smoking' jacket, see-through blouses and safari jackets. Opened a ready-to-wear chain, Rive Gauche, in 1966. In the 1970s he created many stylish designs based on masculine jackets and trousers which perfectly suited the tastes of cosmopolitan women. His vibrantly coloured eveningwear, by contrast, became increasingly romantic and his 1976 collection, showing full skirts, boots, vests and shawls, brought ethnic dressing to haute couture.

Ungaro, Emanuel (Matteolti) 1933–. Designer. Born Aix-en-Provence, France, to Italian parents. Trained in his parents' tailoring firm and then moved to Paris in 1955. Worked for Maison Camps tailors until he joined Balenciaga in 1958. In 1962 moved to Courrèges. Three years later Ungaro founded his own house, producing futuristic designs including angular coats, thigh-high boots and metal bras. In the 1970s his clothes became more supple and in the later part of the decade he was innovative in his combining of textured and patterned materials.

Valentino (Valentino Garavani) 1932–. Designer. Born Voghera, Italy. Attended the Accademia Dell'Arte in Milan and the Chambre Syndicale de la Haute Couture in Paris. Worked for Dessès and Laroche in the early 1950s, before opening his own house in Rome in 1959. In 1962 transferred to Florence, where he was acclaimed for glamorous evening gowns often featuring large bows and ruffles. In the 1970s designed highly successful daywear outfits including knife-pleated skirts and long coats worn over trouser suits. He is also associated with the revival of flamboyant, romantic evening dresses in the late 1970s.

Versace, Gianni 1946–97. Designer. Born Calabria, Italy. Versace moved to Milan in 1972 where he worked freelance for Genny, Complice and Callaghan. During the 1970s developed a reputation for eveningwear and for leather-trimmed knitwear for Callaghan. In 1978 founded his own house. Made sensuous, clinging garments often cut on the bias. Drawing on historical references, he created clothes that were bold, sexy and modern.

Sources for 1970s Fashion

Anderson Black, J.,
and Madge Garland
A History of Fashion, 1975

Baynes, Ken,
and Kate Baynes, eds.
*The Shoe Show: British Shoes
since 1790*, 1979

Cardin, Pierre
*Pierre Cardin: Past, Present and
Future*, 1990

Chenoune, Farid
A History of Men's Fashion, 1993

De Marly, Diana
*Fashion for Men: An Illustrated
History*, 1985

Ewing, Elizabeth
Fur in Dress, 1981

*Dress and Undress: A History of
Women's Underwear*, 1978

*History of 20th Century
Fashion*, 1974

Ginsburg, Madeleine
The Hat: Trends and Traditions,
1990

Hall-Duncan, Nancy
*The History of Fashion
Photography*, 1979

Howell, Georgina
*In Vogue: Six Decades of
Fashion*, 1975

Kennett, Frances
*The Collectors' Book of
Twentieth Century Fashion*, 1983

La Vine, W. Robert
In a Glamorous Fashion, 1981

Lee-Potter, Charlie
Sportswear in Vogue, 1984

Martin, Richard,
and Harold Koda
*Jocks and Nerds: Men's Style in
the Twentieth Century*, 1989

Moke, Johnny, and Jan McVeigh
Mods!, 1979

Mulvagh, Jane
*Vogue: History of 20th Century
Fashion*, 1988

O'Hara, Georgina
The Encyclopaedia of Fashion,
1986

Peacock, John
Costume 1066 to the 1990s,
1994

*The Chronicle of Western
Costume*, 1991

20th Century Fashion, 1993

Men's Fashion, 1996

Probert, Christina
Lingerie in Vogue since 1910,
1981

Robinson, Julian
*The Fine Art of Fashion: An
Illustrated History*, 1989

Simon, Pedro
The Bikini, 1986

Magazines

Burda International, Offenburg,
Germany

Elle, Paris

*Fashion Knits, Paton's Knitwear
Magazine*, Bradford and London

Fashion Weekly Newspaper,
London

Girl about Town, London

G.Q., Gentleman's Quarterly,
London

Harper's Bazaar, Milan

Harpers and Queen, London

*L'Officiel de la couture et de la
mode de Paris*, Paris

L'Uomo Vogue, Milan

Moditalia, Firenze

Nova, IPC Magazines Ltd,
London

19, IPC Magazines Ltd, London

Simplicity Pattern Book, London

*Sir, Men's International Fashion
Journal*, Amsterdam

Vogue, New York

Vogue, London

Vogue, Paris

Vogue Patterns, New York and
London

View, Men's Fashion, London

Woman's Journal, London

Acknowledgments

I would like to thank Liz Salmon,
Assistant Keeper of Arts, Stoke-
on-Trent City Museum and Art
Gallery, for the use of the
Museum's archives and for help
and assistance with my research.

Thanks are also due to the Yale
School of Art and Design,
Wrexham, Clwyd, for the use of
their facilities.